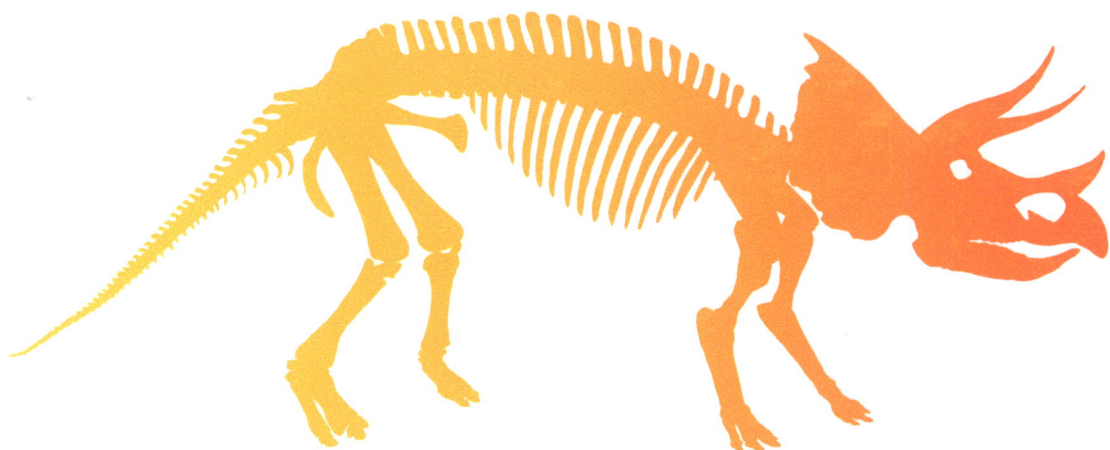

Check out all of the books in the Tell Me About Dinosaurs Series

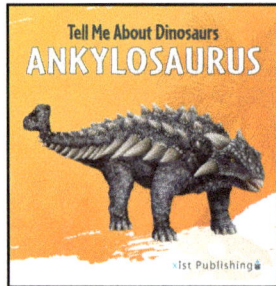

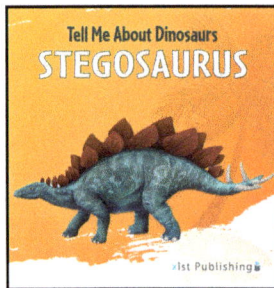

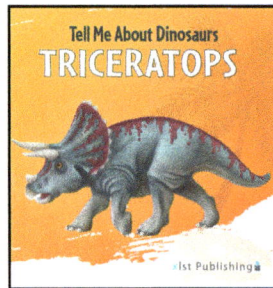

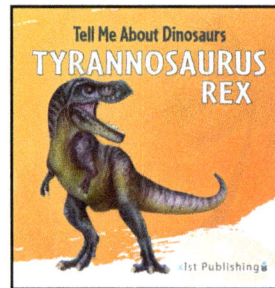

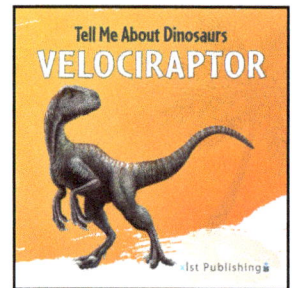

Tell Me About Dinosaurs
ANKYLOSAURUS
Xist Publishing

Tell Me About Dinosaurs
BRACHIOSAURUS
Xist Publishing

Tell Me About Dinosaurs
SPINOSAURUS
Xist Publishing

Tell Me About Dinosaurs
STEGOSAURUS
Xist Publishing

Tell Me About Dinosaurs
TRICERATOPS
Xist Publishing

Tell Me About Dinosaurs
TYRANNOSAURUS REX
Xist Publishing

Tell Me About Dinosaurs
VELOCIRAPTOR
Xist Publishing

Published in the United States by Xist Publishing
www.xistpublishing.com
© 2025 Copyright Xist Publishing

First Edition
Hardcover ISBN: 978-1-5324-5507-0
Paperback ISBN: 978-1-5324-5508-7
eISBN: 978-1-5324-5506-3

PUBLISHED IN TEXAS

Tell Me About Dinosaurs
TRICERATOPS

Marjorie Seevers

x*ist Publishing

10 feet tall

4

30 feet long

Triceratops was a big dinosaur.

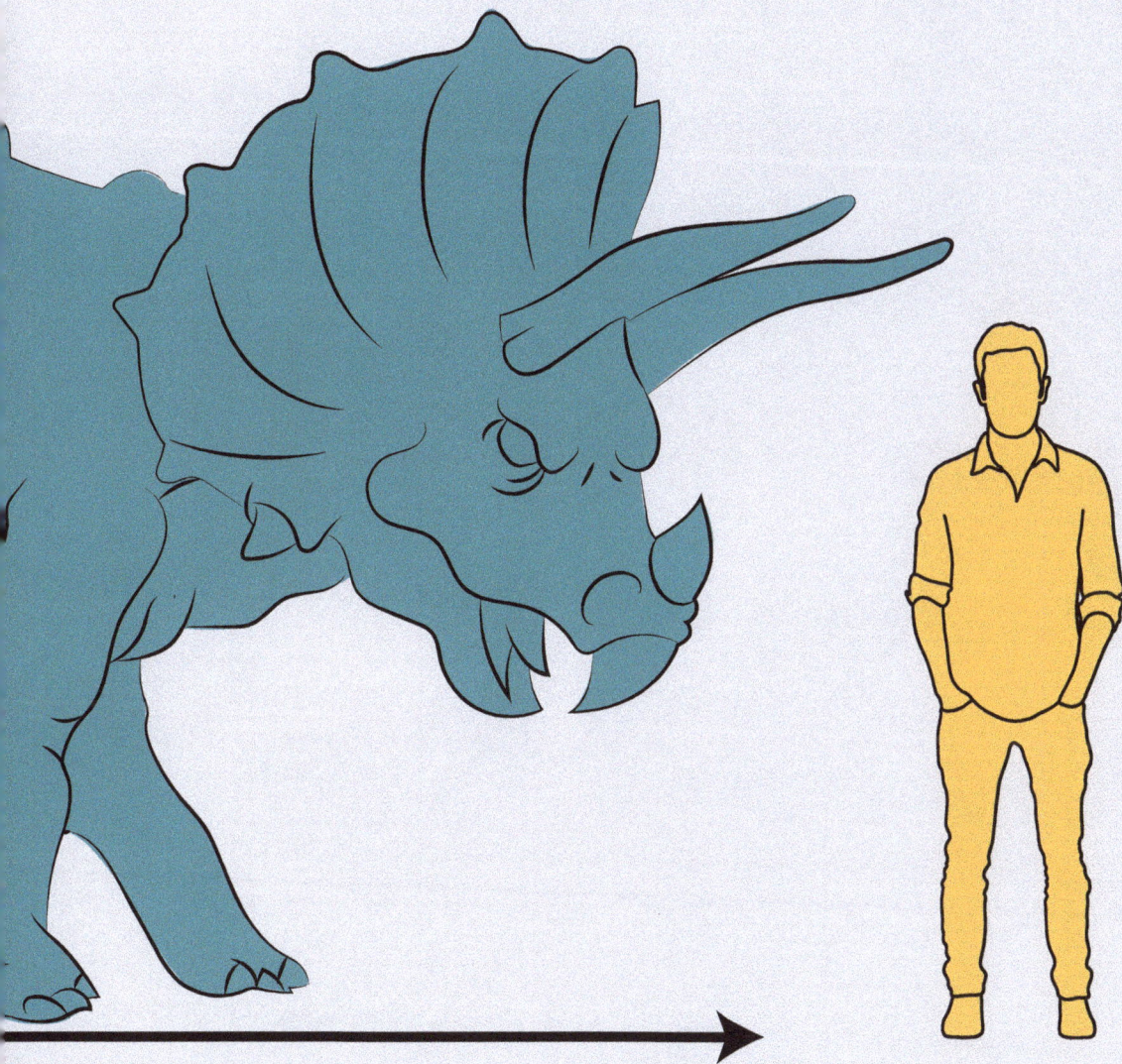

It ate plants.

7

It had three horns
and a beak-like
mouth.

Triceratops had a big frill on the back of its head.

It was very strong.

13

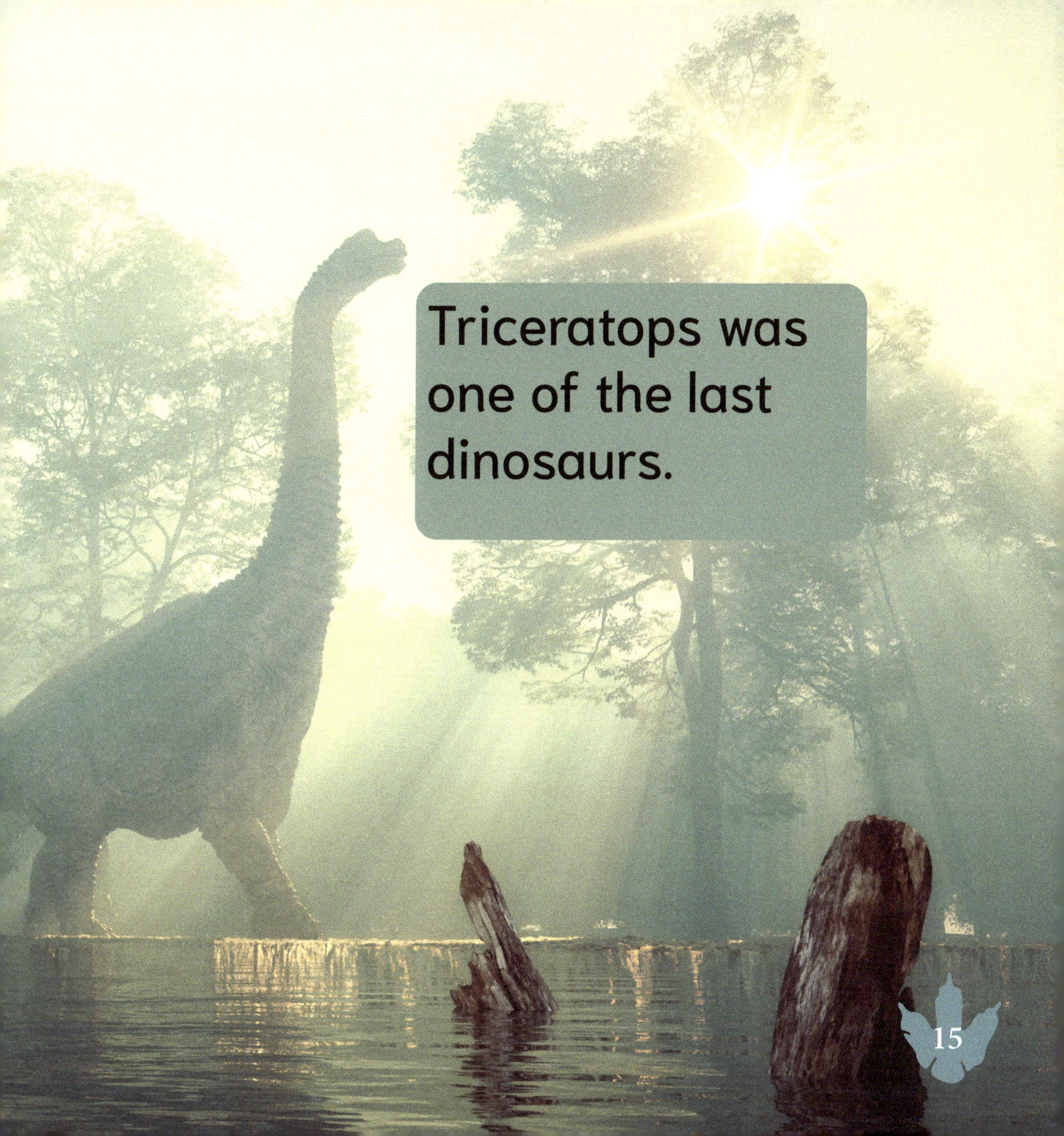

Triceratops was one of the last dinosaurs.

Triceratops bones are
called fossils.

Which dinosaur is a Triceratops?

What did Triceratops eat?